THE QUICK EXPERT'S GUIDE TO
Being a You Tuber

Adam Sutherland

WAYLAND
www.waylandbooks.co.uk

First published in paperback in 2016 by Wayland

Wayland
An imprint of
Hachette Children's Group
Part of Hodder & Stoughton
Carmelite House
50 Victoria Embankment
London EC4Y 0DZ

Editor: Hayley Fairhead
Design: Rocket Design (East Anglia) Ltd
All images and graphic elements: Shutterstock

Dewey classification number: 006.7-dc23

ISBN: 978 0 7502 9776 9
Library e-book ISBN: 978 0 7502 9280 1
10 9 8 7 6 5 4 3 2 1

FSC
www.fsc.org
MIX
Paper from
responsible sources
FSC® C104740

Printed in China

An Hachette UK company
www.hachette.co.uk
www.hachettechildrens.co.uk

>>>CONTENTS<<<

We have highlighted blogs, websites and tools throughout this guide in bold; we didn't want to overload you with URLs, but you should be able to find them really easily through search engines.

TO THE UTTERLY EXCELLENT WORLD OF YOUTUBE!

YouTube is the world's number one entertainment site! From weird and wonderful virals; to amateur vloggers making millions of fans (and millions of pounds) by telling followers about their day; to global broadcasters using the site to launch ground-breaking new entertainment shows and formats; YouTube is undoubtedly THE place to see and be seen.

So how do you become a YouTuber and go from lazy viewer to epic filmmaker? This book will give you essential advice and guidance on every step of the process.

Find out how to start your own YouTube account. Think about what kind of videos you want to create. What do you think the world needs to hear? Learn how to film, edit and upload your clips (even straight from your mobile phone!), customise your channel and boost your online following. Follow our simple steps and you could become the next YouTube sensation!

SO GRAB YOUR VIDEO CAMERA AND SUMMON YOUR INNER FILM DIRECTOR FOR THE QUICK EXPERT TEAM'S SHOW-AND-TELL ON:

Making your videos **stand out** from the crowd

Great lighting, framing, audio and editing **tips**

How to **safely grow** your online followers

Famous YouTubers' tips on building massively popular channels

Using video to **share your interests** with the rest of the world

START YOUR CHANNEL

✳ CREATE AN ACCOUNT

Do you want to make videos that amuse, entertain and inform other people? If you want to be part of the wonderful world of YouTube you've come to the right place. So, let's get started! Right now, we're going to give you a super-quick run-down of the YouTube site so you can get an idea of what goes where and what it all means.

First things first, if you haven't done so already, you should create an account for yourself. This is NOT a channel (that will come later). An account is what cyber whizz-kids call intuitive; it remembers what you have watched and it makes suggestions of other YouTube stuff you might like. Just enter a few details, and you'll be sent a link to verify your email address. Click on that, then add a pic of yourself, a pair of trousers, your cat, or whatever you want as the 'face' of your account, and you're in.

SAY WHAT?

Over 1 billion people visit YouTube every month, watching 6 billion hours of video between them. That's almost an hour for every single person on the planet.

DIY DUDE

Homepage

The YouTube homepage is your entry point into the world of YouTube. At the top of the screen in the middle, there are two headings: **What to Watch** and **My Subscriptions**. (There will be nothing **under My Subscriptions** until you start subscribing to channels.)

Under **What to Watch** you should see:

* **Popular on YouTube** (at the end of the first five video thumbnails is a little forward arrow. Click this to scroll to more suggestions.)

* A number of recommended channels (again, don't forget to use the arrow to scroll).

Next to the YouTube logo in the top left-hand corner of the screen, you will see three horizontal red lines with a down arrow next to them. Click the down arrow and it will change your view of the YouTube menu. You will now see a list of options below the YouTube logo:

* **My Channel** (read on, we're coming to that)

* **My Subscriptions** (a list of the other YouTube channels you are following)

* **History** (a way for you to look back at what you've been watching if you want to recommend something to a friend, or go back and watch it again)

* **Watch Later** (for videos you have tagged to remind yourself to come back and view).

✻ WATCH SOME VIDEOS

If you haven't done so already, it's well worth spending some time watching some videos. Not only is it lots of fun, it will also give you loads of inspiration to become a YouTuber yourself! It should also help you start to decide what kind of videos you want to make, and just as importantly, what kind of videos you DON'T want to make.

✻ WHAT'S THE RIGHT CHANNEL FOR YOU?

Answering these five tough questions will give you a great idea about the sort of YouTuber you want to be.

1. What's already out there?

People use YouTube for a massive variety of things, such as watching Premiership goals, learning new skills with tutorial videos, enjoying daft viral videos, watching music videos... the list goes on. Think about what you can bring to viewers that they aren't getting from anyone else.

2. What are your strengths?

If you enjoy making your friends laugh, think about recording some comedy videos. If you're an X Factor wannabee, maybe upload some videos of you performing? The most important thing is to create content that will keep your viewers coming back for more.

3. Could you offer expert advice?

Are you interested in films? Music? The latest gadgets? Reviews are a great way to gain viewers. Lots of people search out reviews before going out to buy something — from headphones to lipstick to shampoo. Think about one of these areas to review: new music releases, films and tv shows, computer games, health and beauty, healthy-eating recipes, fashion on a budget…

4. How much time do you have?

We'll talk about how often you should be updating your videos later, but you should also bear in mind how long they will take to film and edit. The more complicated they are, the longer they will take. If you have exams coming up, it would be a good idea to start with something simple: you talking to camera, telling jokes, reviewing films, giving healthy-eating tips. The filming and editing time for these clips would be much shorter than some of the more complicated channels with several people and lots of different locations. The more complicated and time-consuming your channel is to update, the more likely you are to let release dates of new videos slip because of other commitments. Start simply, and build an audience.

SAY WHAT?

" I'd love to say that there is [a] specific thing someone could do [to be a successful YouTuber]. But I think the main thing that really makes it work is that, if you're having fun, being yourself and filming something that you would watch yourself, it becomes contagious for other people to watch too. "

Zoella, 2014, Company *magazine*

https://www.youtube.com/user/pixiwoo

https://www.youtube.com/user/smosh

5. Are you going solo?

Do you want to make a solo channel or something with a friend or friends? Pixiwoo and Smosh are great examples of partnerships that work really well. Perhaps you have a friend who makes a great double act with you? Sometimes this will give you more confidence to stand in front of the camera. It also shares the workload if you don't have much time. Just remember to work with someone you get on well with!

✳ HOW TO PRESENT YOUR VIDEOS

Now you've thought about what type of channel is right for you, it's time to think about how to present your videos. Read on for some ideas.

Video blog (vlog) and video diaries

Vlogs and video diaries are a huge part of YouTube's success. A series of One Direction video diaries hit between 5-7 million views each! Don't expect your video to hit those figures — not straight away, at least! — but a video blog is a great way to get subscribers to your channel, as viewers will regularly visit your channel for updates on the ups and downs of your life.

Goofy pets

Come on, admit it — we've all watched them. Cats falling off the bed, dogs dancing on two legs… animal videos are watched by millions of YouTube viewers. If you have an entertaining pet (we're thinking opera-singing poodle), why not share it with the world?

Video mashups

A mashup is a collection of clips edited together, such as 20 great World Cup goals, people sneezing live on television, or a collection of short clips from music videos. For the 2008 US Presidential Election, Barack Obama fans made a mashup called 'Vote Different'. So maybe a mashup even helped President Obama into the White House.

Web series

A video series can be a little more complicated to create, but if you see yourself becoming an actor, writer or director, it's certainly a great place to start learning your skills. Most web series are funny, and include a hook at the end of every episode (sorry, webisode) to get viewers coming back for the next instalment. There are some great examples from producer Epic Robot TV.

https://www.youtube.com/user/EpicRobotTV

>> THE BOFFIN BIT <<

THE MARKET

The 'market' for your channel is the potential number of viewers that your channel will appeal to. If you run a channel on gaming reviews, for example, you are appealing to an estimated market of 1.2 billion gamers around the world. Phew! If you launch a channel devoted to Grimsby Town Athletics Club, your market will be considerably smaller. Think about what you want to achieve before you start. The most successful YouTubers appeal to the widest possible audience, but that doesn't mean you can't be quirky, fun or oddball! Because YouTube's audience is so huge, every kind of 'niche market' (in other words, a group of people sharing the same obscure interest) can be catered for.

How-to videos

If you're a gifted guitar player, a well-practised ballet dancer or great at football keepie-uppies, why not share your skills with a series of 'How-to' videos? Millions of YouTubers are doing it, and millions more are watching. Remember, reduce the advice down to one simple chord sequence, dance move or trick per video. It gives you the opportunity to build up a library of videos, and gives viewers the chance to go away and master what they've learned, then come back for more.

✳ CREATING YOUR CHANNEL

Now you've thought through what channel you want to create and the types of videos you want to make, it's time to set up your own channel. Not surprisingly, YouTube makes it as easy as possible for you to start your own channel. Visit **https://www.youtube.com/yt/about/en-GB/getting-started.html** and under the section **Make Your Own Channel** click the blue box: **Create a Channel**.

This will take you to **https://www.youtube.com/channel_switcher**

Click the left-hand box with a big **+** sign called **Create a New Channel** and you will be taken to a page with a blank box entitled **Name Your Channel**.

Now you need to come up with a name for your channel. Choose something distinctive and original to make your channel stand out from the crowd. Most YouTubers use nicknames or obscure usernames that hide their real identity, such as PewDiePie (see page 45). It's a good idea to do this too.

From the next dropdown menu, choose a category for your videos, such as **Arts**, **Entertainment** or **Sports**. Tick the box about agreeing to the terms (once you've looked at the terms and conditions of course!) and click Finished. You now have your channel!

At this stage, you might want to accept the invitation to **Take a Tour of Your New Channel**.

Once you've clicked on **Next**, you'll see the **Activity Feed**. This shows your uploaded videos and other public activity.

✳ CUSTOMISE YOUR CHANNEL

Go to **Add Channel Art** where you can customise the look of your channel by adding some artwork. Have a look at how some of your favourite YouTubers customise the look of their channels. You can use your own images, or choose from a (limited) gallery. We recommend using your own pics for a look that's really your own.

Your YouTube channel will be viewable on everything from a desktop computer to a SMART TV to a mobile. Depending on the art you choose, it may look different from one device to the next. YouTube will show you how it will look, and give you the chance to adjust the crop on pics before you confirm. Use artwork that will draw your viewer's attention. The cover image will set your channel apart from the rest of the YouTube interface. Include your channel's name or a message in the channel art. This will help solidify your name in the viewer's mind.

Unless you want to set a brand image by keeping the same picture, consider regularly changing your channel art in relation to what content you are releasing on your channel. For example, if you are doing comedy sketches, change the channel art so that it relates to your current set of sketches.

For tips on customising your channel art, visit **https://support.google.com/youtube/answer/2972003?topic=16630&ctx=topic&hl=en-GB**

REALITY CHECK

OFFICIAL REALITY CHECKER

THIS CARD CERTIFIES THAT
Melvin
IS OFFICIALLY APPOINTED TO CHECK REALITY ON BEHALF OF THE QUICK EXPERT'S GUIDE

☑ Tanya Burr

https://www.youtube.com/user/pixiwoo

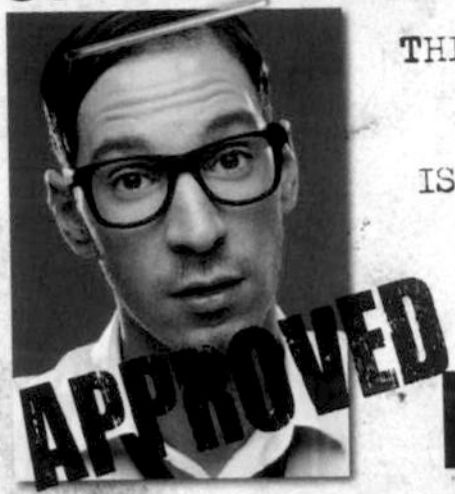

Norfolk-born Tanya Burr left school at 16, did a short make-up course, and started work on the beauty counter of her local department store. When she got home, she would post step-by-step make-up tutorials on YouTube. "Early on they were mainly celebrities' looks... how to create famous faces," she says.

Two years later, Burr left her job to devote herself to her blog and tutorials full-time. Burr's influence over fans' buying habits has made her an important ally to fashion brands. A Mulberry handbag she featured in one video caused the Mulberry website to be bombarded with hits, and resulted in an invite for Burr to the Mulberry show at London Fashion Week. But Burr keeps her feet on the ground, "The most important thing is to give viewers what they want and to keep the videos unique and professional."

OFFICIAL FORM C-185/A

Describe your channel

Adding a brief description to your channel helps the viewer understand quickly what kind of content to expect. To adjust the channel description, click the **About** tab in the main channel window. From there click on **Channel Description**.

You can also use the **Channel Description** section to update news about your channel, and even discuss who appears in your videos. For example, you might want to say 'Working with best friends Katie and Paul to record some new fun videos', or 'Just uploaded five new videos of make-up tips'.

Adding links

You'll see that you can also add links — perhaps to a website or another social media page. For example, add a link to a YouTube collection of Cristiano Ronaldo free kicks — or his official website, Twitter page and so on — if you are doing a 'Take a free kick like Ronaldo' video. Be careful not to include links to your own personal social media pages, or any other personal information like phone numbers etc. If you're going to set up social media relating to your channel, use the same name as your channel for consistency and safety (see page 54).

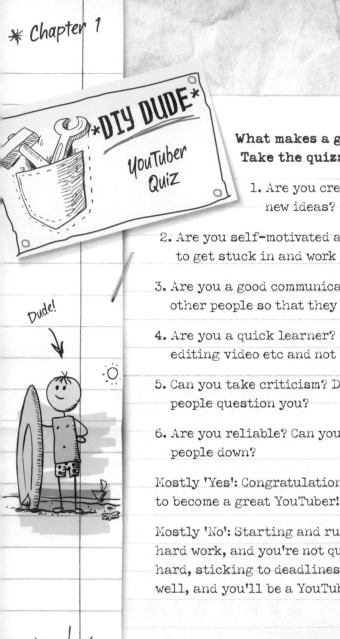

DIY DUDE
YouTuber Quiz

What makes a good YouTuber? Take the quiz:

1. Are you creative? Do you enjoy dreaming up new ideas?

2. Are you self-motivated and hard working? Are you prepared to get stuck in and work long hours if necessary?

3. Are you a good communicator? Can you explain things to other people so that they understand them?

4. Are you a quick learner? Can you tackle new skills like editing video etc and not be scared off?

5. Can you take criticism? Do you believe in yourself if other people question you?

6. Are you reliable? Can you keep to deadlines and not let people down?

Mostly 'Yes': Congratulations, you definitely have what it takes to become a great YouTuber!

Mostly 'No': Starting and running your own YouTube channel is hard work, and you're not quite there yet. But keep on working hard, sticking to deadlines, being creative and communicating well, and you'll be a YouTuber in no time!

Dude!

The YouTube Partner Programme helps over a million video creators from more than 30 countries earn money from their videos every month through advertising.

SAY WHAT?

QUICK EXPERT SUMMARY

Think about what channel is right for you before you start.
Ask yourself questions such as:

- What am I good at? And what would I enjoy doing?

- What kind of channels do people want to watch?

- How much time can I devote to it?

- Do I want to work alone or with a friend?

- How do I improve on what's already out there? What will make my channel unique?

LIGHTS, CAMERA, ACTION

✳ FIVE STEPS TO MAKING GREAT VIDEOS

OK, so here's where we talk you through picking up a camera and actually recording some video. No one's expecting you to be making clips worthy of BBC3 or MTV — most YouTubers are enthusiastic amateurs, and the 'homemade' feel of your videos can add to their charm. Read our essential pointers to making your videos the best they can possibly be!

1. Be yourself

However much you're tempted to put on a posh voice or try to impress people with your 'serious' delivery, viewers will be able to tell in less than ten seconds whether you're being genuine in your videos.

What are you really like: funny, bubbly, serious, a joker or a brainbox? Whatever your personality might be, show it off in your videos. In the same way you'd be yourself with your family and friends, you need to be like that in your videos. Anything else, and viewers will quickly look elsewhere.

Along the same lines, don't copy other people's styles. OK, so you love Zoella — so do Zoella's fans, and they'll go to Zoella's channel to see her — not your channel! For you to attract your own viewers, you need to figure out what's original about you and play it up.

https://www.youtube.com/user/zoella280390

Expect to be nervous the first few times you make a video. One good tip from the pros is to try imagining the camera as the face of your best friend. Joke around or get serious, the same as you would with someone you're mates with.

And don't be worried about embarrassing yourself! If you get your words mixed up a little, or try a joke that's pretty lame, your viewers will relate to you even more because they'll see you as human. You are human, right? Just checking.

2. Speak up

Just like you would in front of any audience, you need to speak clearly and make eye contact with your YouTube audience. This will hold your viewers' attention and make your videos much more interesting to watch. Look directly into the camera, don't mumble, and your viewers won't grumble...

3. Focus on quality

No one's expecting your video to be perfect (this is YouTube, after all), but if it has terrible lighting and bad sound, people are going to click away quickly. Good video quality means using a decent video camera. This doesn't have to cost hundreds of pounds (see pages 22-23). Most smartphones these days come with pretty good video features. But no matter which video camera you're using, the following tips will instantly improve the quality of your videos.

⦿ Shooting indoors? Turn the lights on! Sounds obvious, but you'd be surprised how many people forget. This will not only brighten your picture, but also make everything look more colourful and interesting.

◉ You don't need to look like you're filming under floodlights: experiment with turning on lights placed in various parts of the room (it's called ambient lighting, if you want to sound posh) and see how it changes the look of your videos. Oh, and make sure your face is clearly visible, even if the background isn't.

◉ Eliminate background noises as much as possible. Turn off the TV, ask your dad to stop hoovering... you get the idea. Background noises lower the quality of your video.

◉ If you're talking to the camera, make sure that the camera is steady (see page 23)! You might be giving viewers the secret to living to 120, but nobody is going to watch it if your camera's shaking.

>> THE BOFFIN BIT <<

YOUTUBE RANKING

Individual videos and YouTube channels are 'ranked' by how long users spend viewing them. If the majority of users watch your video all the way through, it will do better in the search rankings. So, when a user searches for a video on the subject you have covered, the link to your video will appear nearer the top in the search ranking. (Think Google search rankings. How often do you click the first three or four entries and forget the rest?) Always think about how long your videos will last when you are making them!

4. Plan your videos in advance

Every video essentially needs to tell a story. There should be a beginning, middle and end. This is as true for a comedy sketch as it is for a tutorial on shaping your eyebrows.

The introduction to your video needs to be attention-grabbing. Most viewers will determine a video's worth in the first few seconds, so work hard on making your intros fun and informative. The longer viewers watch your video, the higher YouTube will rank your videos on search results.

Talk directly to the audience. Introduce the video, briefly discussing what to expect. If you're making a review or tutorial video, make sure that the purpose is clear at the very beginning. For example, "Hi guys, today I'm going to tell you about how to blow the biggest bubblegum bubble ever...". If this is what viewers want, they'll know straight away not to look for another, more informative video.

Break up long videos into segments that focus on different aspects of the topic, and release them one at a time. So, if your video is about how to get the top score on a particular video game, you might focus on the four or five hardest parts of the game that people most often get stuck on and show viewers how to get through the different parts in separate videos. Shorter videos make the content more digestible — and more memorable — for the viewer.

Once your editing improves, you can show a teaser of clips from the video that the viewer is about to watch. (See pages 37—41 for more editing tips.)

5. Practice makes perfect!

Film as often as possible. Not only will a steady stream of content keep your audience glued to your channel, it will also help you improve as you continue to develop your style.

21

SAY WHAT?

" What I do [is] almost like hanging around and watching your [friend] play video games. My fans care... about what they are watching. "

Felix Kjellberg, aka PewDiePie

✳ CHOOSING THE RIGHT CAMERA

Not surprisingly, the camera you choose will have a major effect, not only on how you record your videos, but also on the quality of your end results.

Deciding what kind of videos you're going to make (see pages 10–11) is an important step. For example, if you plan to record video diaries/a vlog, your computer's built-in webcam, or a standalone webcam, could be enough. If you're planning a web series, a better camera with a wider range of features will help you get more professional results.

Budget will probably be the main factor in your decision, but make sure you find a camera that is easy to use and, hopefully, flexible enough for your future needs.

◉ **WEBCAM £**
Pros: Widely available, cheap, good for vlogs and video diaries.
Cons: Basic lens means low-quality images. Connection to computer means you have to stay in front of, or close to, your computer to use it.

◉ SMARTPHONE £

Pros: Widely available (you may already have one!), lots of other uses.

Cons: Again, sound and lighting quality will be average at best. Battery life will be short.

◉ DIGITAL CAMERA ££

Pros: Light, portable.

Cons: Needs good ambient lighting (or look for a camera with low-light features), limited picture quality.

◉ CAMCORDER £££

Pros: Great picture and sound quality, portability, range of features (zoom, playback etc).

Cons: Cost, better picture quality (HD) and more features than you may need — at least at first.

✳ TOP TEN FILMING TIPS

You've chosen your camera, planned your video and now it's time to start shooting. You don't have to be the next Quentin Tarantino to gain viewers on YouTube. Just follow our tips for the top, and you'll be shooting great videos in no time!

1. Holding the camera

Yes, it sounds simple, but what we really mean is 'don't hold the camera'! In other words, use a tripod whenever possible. And don't be jerky: any movements of the camera should be as slow and smooth as possible. Moving swiftly from side to side or up and down will make your viewers feel seasick! If you do have to hold the camera, stand with your feet apart to give a steady base. Put your right hand through the camera's sidegrip (if you're using a camcorder), and keep your right elbow against your body — again, for stability. If your camera has an image stabilisation feature (called SteadyShot or OIS), this will also minimise camera shake.

2. Focusing

Automatic focus is the simplest way to get sharp, professional-looking video. Avoid changing lighting conditions if you're using autofocus, as the camera sometimes takes time to lock onto a subject — particularly in low light. The same goes for distance: try to stay the same distance from your subject, as moving forwards or backwards could have your camera 'hunting' — that's searching for focus, to you non-camcorder boffins.

When you're ready, have a go at manual focus. It can cope with multiple subjects so you can choose what you want in focus, whereas automatic focus will just choose the person closest to the camera. Low light conditions, bright light sources, and movement within the frame are also no problem when you're using manual focus.

The best way to make sure you're focusing correctly is to zoom in close to your subject, make sure the focus is sharp, then zoom back out to reframe the shot (more on framing later). Some 'prosumer' cameras (the more expensive end of consumer cameras and camcorders) will have a 'push focus' button, which uses the camera's automatic focus to lock onto a subject before returning controls to manual. Clever!

3. Understanding exposure

Setting exposure (how light or dark your video looks) is the trickiest thing you'll need to master on your camera. Firstly, there are three controls to think about: shutter, aperture and gain (sensitivity). Put your camera into auto mode, and it will take care of all three for you, but there will be times when you'll find it preferable — even necessary — to have manual control. For example, a camera using automatic exposure may change exposure if you move the camera slightly to the right or the left of your subject to get a different angle to shoot from.

4. Setting up a shot

There are several kinds of shots you can use to produce a great-looking YouTube video:

Wide shot (or Long Shot)

A wide shot (WS) frames action from a distance, and is good for creating an 'establishing shot' that usually comes at the beginning of a sequence — to show the location you're filming in, for example. Wide shots are rarely used for YouTube videos, however, as it's hard to view much detail on a laptop or smartphone screen. Avoid unless absolutely necessary (like if you're filming on the top of the Grand Canyon maybe?!).

Full shot

A full shot (FS) frames the entire subject – like a shot of a person from head to toe. Like the wide shot, it's not often used for YouTube videos, but if you want to show scale, relative sizes, or something interesting/ funny about a person – maybe they're stilt-walking? – then a full shot's the one to use.

Medium shot

A medium shot (MS) is usually framed from the waist up. Medium shots are great for capturing a person's gestures, and are regularly used for YouTube videos as they're far enough away to help the subject tell the story, and close enough to cut out unnecessary background details.

Close-up

The close-up (or CU) is probably the most widely used shot for web video as it brings the subject closer to the viewer, and reveals much more information (e.g. a person's facial expressions and mood) within a limited space. Close-ups are usually framed from the neck up when a person is talking to camera, but can also show feet (for dancing tutorials, for example), or hands (for card tricks). Close-ups also look great in YouTube's small video player windows.

5. Zooming

If you want great-looking video, avoid zooming while shooting – it will make you look like a beginner. Instead, use your zoom to reframe a shot, especially if you're shooting from a distance. In other words, imagine you're showing a card trick as a medium shot, and then you do a close-up shot on just the magician's hands. Most cameras have zoom controls with a 'W' for wide shots and a 'T' for tight shots. Experiment, and decide which works best for your shot.

6. Angles and camera height

As well as your shot selection, the angle and height of your camera will have a major impact on the videos you create. Experimenting with camera placement can achieve some great results! Here are the most common shots you can use:

Eye level

This is probably the most common shot used in YouTube videos, when the subject of the video speaks directly to the camera. Placing a camera at eye level helps the subject of the video 'communicate' more easily with the viewer.

High angle

High angles are shots looking down at the subject, and can make the subject look less threatening. Some YouTubers achieve this effect with webcams mounted on top of their desktop computers.

Low angle

Low angles are shots looking up at a subject from below. They can make the subject look taller or scarier, and can make the viewer feel small and unimportant. Unless you're making a short film, you probably won't use this one very often.

Oblique angle

This is an angle that's tilted to create an unusual perspective — maybe with the subject in profile, or upside down. For a 'dog's eye view' on the subject, consider placing your camera at a very low height.

7. Framing your subject

You're well on the way to becoming an A-grade YouTuber! The next thing to consider is composing, or framing, an image — in other words, where in the frame (that is, the rectangle of your camera screen) the image sits. Here are a few golden rules to remember.

27

The rule of thirds

Think of your frame/screen as divided into nine equally sized parts, with two vertical lines, and two horizontal lines dividing it. Wherever the lines join is what's called a 'point of interest', so placing a subject's eyes at one of those points, for example, can create a strong composition. If you're filming outside, it's also a good idea to place the horizon at either the bottom third or the top third of the frame.

The 180 degree rule

This sounds a bit mathematical, but stay with us! Let's say you're filming a friend interviewing someone about their favourite pizza toppings. Draw an imaginary line between the two subjects in your frame, and make sure you stay one side of that line. In other words, don't go round and film from the other side — the subject and the interviewee would be switched and everyone would start getting confused! You should also follow this rule if, for example, you're filming someone going through a door. Imagine you have a door on the left-hand side of your screen, and someone walking towards it from right to left across the screen. They open the door and step into it. If your next frame shows the door opening from the other side and the person stepping through it, they need to carry on walking right to left when they come through the door.

8. Camera movement

We've mentioned before that any camera movement needs to be slow and deliberate, and only used from time to time. Nevertheless, there are times when some movement will add interest to your videos. Here are two moves to try.

Panning and tilting

Panning is the motion of turning a camera from side to side on its centre axis. Imagine your camera is on a tripod and you have a football team lined up in front of you. You start at one end, and swivel the camera round to the other end — that's panning. If you don't have a tripod, turning at the waist will give the same effect. Pan as slowly as possible to avoid motion blur (which is what it sounds like). Tilting is the up and down version of a pan. You could use it to show the size of a REALLY tall building, for example.

Dolly

Smoothly moving the camera closer or further away from your subject is called a dolly move. In proper films, the camera is mounted on a kind of wheeled cart. You'll get a similar effect by walking VERY carefully backwards or forwards. Use two hands to hold your camera, keep your eyes on the view screen and stay as steady as you can.

REALITY CHECK

OFFICIAL REALITY CHECKER

THIS CARD CERTIFIES THAT
Melvin
IS OFFICIALLY APPOINTED
TO CHECK REALITY ON
BEHALF OF THE QUICK
EXPERT'S GUIDE

APPROVED

☑ Jamal Edwards

At 14 years old, Londoner Jamal Edwards started recording videos of foxes raiding the dustbins outside the tower block where he lived.

By 15 he was following the grime music scene, filming rappers performing for his Smokey Barz TV channel (now SB.TV Music). Today, the 24-year-old has interviewed Prime Minister David Cameron, is credited by music artists Jessie J and Rita Ora as helping to launch their careers, and is worth an estimated £8 million.

Edwards puts his success down to hard work and ambition. "I was always trying to expand. I could have just stayed in West London, but [I went] east, north, south, central! I was uploading a video every day. I'd finish college, and I'd be editing my videos on the way home [to get] my clip online first."

9. Lighting

We know you're working with zero budget — never fear, there are lots of ways to improve the lighting in your video that cost nothing, or next to nothing. Here are a few dos and don'ts.

◉ **DON'T** position your subject with their back to a window. Your camera will adjust exposure to allow for the light coming through the window, and your subject will look dark and underexposed. Instead place them opposite, or at an angle to, the window — that way, they will catch the light on their face.

◉ **DO** place your subject facing the sun when shooting outdoors. Filming around midday in bright sunshine will create long, dark shadows on your subject's face. Avoid these with a reflector (a big round piece of silver material that reflects light). Don't have a reflector? Try to shoot earlier or later in the day when the shadows are reduced.

◉ **DO** make use of light sources when filming inside. Standing your subject next to a table lamp could give you a great effect, for example.

◉ **DON'T** spend money on expensive lighting. Use what's around you, and experiment!

◉ **DO** keep an eye on your camera's white balance. Believe it or not, light has many different colours. Outdoor light is bluer, whereas indoor light is generally more orange. Your camcorder should deal with this automatically, but to be sure try this: choose an indoor or outdoor light setting (depending on where you are), point the camera at a white surface (a sheet of paper will do), and press the white balance button — this adjusts the camera's white balance to your current environment. (Consult your camera's manual for specific instructions.)

10. Recording audio

Audio is often the most overlooked aspect of any video shoot, but it's crucial — at least if you want viewers to hear what you're saying! There are two ways to record better audio.

I. Controlling your environment

◉ Avoid a location with background noise — standing on the side of a motorway, or under an airport flight path is not a good idea!

>> THE BOFFIN BIT <<

SOUND RECORDING

There are two types of sound – sync and non-sync. Sync sound means it 'syncs', or matches, the movements of someone's lips when they are talking, or the sound of hands clapping. Non-sync sound is, for example, the mixture of sounds you'll hear on your high street – cars driving past, dogs barking, people talking. If you record sound separately, you can 'layer' it over the video to improve what you're hearing. For example, if you are recording a video of you interviewing people on a busy high street, you would hear the sounds of your voice and the interviewee's voice most prominently, but you would also hear the sound of passing cars etc more faintly in the background. If you're adding music, or even talking over a scene to explain what you are going to do, think about the relative importance of each sound, and layer them accordingly. Remember: the better the sound, the better the video!

◉ Don't use big, echo-y, empty rooms — sound will bounce around in there and sound awful, awful, awful...

◉ If possible, when you're using a microphone, also wear headphones when recording. It's the best way to properly judge audio levels as you record.

2. Choosing the right equipment

Believe it or not, the microphone on your camcorder is often the worst microphone for the job. Not only is it low quality, it's also designed to pick up audio from all different directions at once (called 'omnidirectional'). So you not only get the voice you want, but all the background noises that you don't!

To record great audio, you'll need a separate directional microphone. If you can afford it, try one of these:

◉ Shotgun microphone £

Not designed to capture audio over a long distance, but great when your subject is just a few feet away. Eliminates excess noise from the side and behind. Can be mounted on top of your camera.

◉ Lavalier microphone ££

A small, light microphone that can clip onto your subject's collar etc. Reduces outside noise simply because it's so close to the subject's mouth. Great for other sound effects — for example, can be clipped on a trouser leg to get the sound of footsteps.

◉ Handheld microphone £££

Great if you're interviewing people on the street when you need to hear the question and the response. Be warned, you may need an adaptor to connect a handheld microphone to your camcorder.

DIY DUDE

Problem solving!

The best way to make great YouTube video is to practise, practise, practise! Try these different scenarios, and work out how to solve the problems they raise.

✳ You're filming an interview between two people – one is 1.8m tall, the other is 1.2m tall. How would you frame the shot? What microphone would you use?

✳ You want to film a clip of a great breakdancer. Think about the range of different shots you could use to show her movements and tricks. What audio would you use?

✳ You want to film in your garden, to show how to tell different plants by their leaves. In terms of light, what would be the best times of day to film? What microphone would you use?

QUICK EXPERT SUMMARY

🔩 What kind of videos are you going to make – vlogs? Web series?

🔩 Plan your videos in advance. Think about what you're going to say. Remember to be yourself!

🔩 Focus on quality – videos should be well lit, with minimal camera shake and good sound quality.

🔩 Choose the right equipment for the job – from cameras to microphones.

🔩 Understand the principles of framing. Set up your shots carefully.

🔩 Expensive equipment doesn't make great videos! Well thought out, entertaining videos are far more important.

MAKING THE CUT

✳ CAPTURING

You've had fun filming some truly amazing videos. Now here's where the (kind of) technical stuff starts. Don't be put off! Millions of video creators capture and edit video every day. There's nothing to it.

Capturing (in other words, downloading) video from your camera to your computer is as simple as plugging the camera into your laptop, desktop PC or Mac. For any problems, there are dozens of video tutorials online (many on YouTube!) to help you.

✳ CHOOSING YOUR EDITING SOFTWARE

Before you start to assemble your video, you'll need software that allows you to work with the video clips you've created. The software we've recommended here is suitable for beginners and, in most cases, already preinstalled on your PC or Mac. It's worth saying here that it's always best to start by using free technology when you're starting out — it's more than adequate for beginners, and you may never feel the need to upgrade even when you get the millionth subscriber to your channel!

For PC

1. **Windows Movie Maker** is the editing software chosen by most PC users. It's basic, but a good place to start. There are also a few useful add-ons you can download to increase the features.

You can download it for free **http://windows.microsoft.com/en-gb/ windows-live/movie-maker**

There are a range of tutorials available on the Microsoft site to help you get used to the programme.

http://windows.microsoft.com/en-gb/windows-vista/getting-started-with-windows-movie-maker

2. **Adobe Premiere Elements** offers users better control and more features than Movie Maker but is around £65 to buy. It's easy to use and — thankfully — not confusing to look at. For more information, visit **http://www.adobe.com/uk/products/premiere-elements.html**

Make sure you keep your computer software updated so you have the latest edition of the software you're using. This is essential if you want the newest features and functionality. To check which version of Windows Movie Maker you are running, start the application, click the **Help** menu drop-down arrow, and choose **About Windows Movie Maker** to check the version number. Latest downloads are available at **www.microsoft.com/downloads**

> **" We look at YouTube trends – challenges, pranks, or whatever. We won't simply follow everything, but we will look at how we can be a part of it. "**
>
> *Ian Hecox, one half of YouTuber Smosh*

SAY WHAT?

https://www.youtube.com/user/smosh

For Mac

1. **iMovie** is one of the iLife suite of applications supplied with every new Mac computer (in other words, it's free!). The layout is simple, and it's nice and easy to use — probably the simplest editing application available on any computer system. Even a complete beginner can be editing videos in minutes, but it's also sophisticated enough to edit full-length, low-budget films. Visit **www.apple.co.uk/ilife** for more information.

REALITY CHECK

OFFICIAL REALITY CHECKER

THIS CARD CERTIFIES THAT
Melvin

IS OFFICIALLY APPOINTED TO CHECK REALITY ON BEHALF OF THE QUICK EXPERT'S GUIDE

APPROVED

☑ Videogame superstar

Olajide Olatunji (better known as YouTuber KSI) started a YouTube account in July 2009, commentating on a FIFA video game. Five years later, he has over 6 million subscribers to his channel, with nearly one billion views!

"I always felt there [were] some goals and tricks that I was doing [on FIFA that were] cool enough to show people on the Internet," he says. From there, the YouTuber started adding funny voiceover commentary to FIFA and other games, and he has now expanded his channel into filming comedy clips. He has even collaborated with rapper Sway on a top 40 hit called 'No Sleep'.

http://ksiolajidebt.com

https://www.youtube.com/user/KSIOlajidebt

2. **Final Cut Express** is a step up from iMovie, in the same way as Adobe Premiere Elements is a step up from Movie Maker. Editing tools are more advanced, and there are additional features, including colour correction. The software is no longer available through Apple (it has been replaced by the more expensive Final Cut Pro), but is still available elsewhere for around £60 from online retailers.

✳ EDITING

Now it's time to start editing! Ask any filmmaker and they'll tell you that editing is a massively important part of the process of making great, watchable videos. A well-edited video will make a much stronger impression on viewers than a quickly thrown-together collection of clips, so spend some time learning the ins and outs of your video editing software.

We won't talk exhaustively about the technical side of editing — expert advice on using your chosen software can be found online and in the Help section of whatever programme you're using. Instead, we're going to give you our Quick Expert's Guide to Making Exciting Videos on YouTube, from cutting to adding special effects, text and graphics.

Match cutting

As the name suggests, match cutting links together action from one shot to the next as seamlessly as possible. It gives the impression that an action continues across two shots — for example, a close-up of a hand picking up a glass of water, and then a medium shot of someone drinking it. The idea is that viewers don't even notice they're watching different shots rather than one continuous one. That way, they focus on the video and don't notice the editing.

Jump cuts

These are cuts that jump from one scene to the next in a slightly odd and jerky way. Unlike match cutting, these can't help but catch your eye, and at worst can be distracting. Nevertheless, they can still be useful. Vloggers use them to cut out the boring bits of a diary entry, and you'll see them in documentaries or sporting highlights when a long sequence needs to be shortened. *Match of the Day* is made up of jump cuts, for example, as they cut out several minutes of boring play between goals.

Split edits

You'll often see split edits used with interviews and dialogue scenes. For example, if the camera shows one person being interviewed, and another person (usually off camera) as the interviewer, you might hear a question from the interviewer while looking at the interviewee. Mixing dialogue and images from different shots avoids flicking backwards and forwards between the two people, and actually 'smooths over' a cut from one shot to the next. The continuing audio helps you not notice the cut.

Applying transitions and special effects

Used properly, these can improve your video no end — from smoothing over cuts, to matching colours and adding text (for example, an on-screen title for your vlog). Don't overdo it, though: use a dissolve or fade out an image to show the passing of time or the move from one location to another, but not for every scene!

AudioSwap

The Audioswap feature on YouTube allows you to replace the audio track on your video with officially licensed music. Rather than use a song without an artist's permission (which is illegal!), you can use a track already licensed by YouTube. Most songs come from smaller musicians who can benefit from lots of people hearing their music. Remember to keep a backup of your original video and audio files, as replacing your audio with Audioswap will permanently delete your audio files. ←

Adding thumbnails

When your video has finished uploading, you're able to choose a thumbnail — basically your video's 'front cover' from the three options that YouTube automatically generates. To select the one you want to use, click the thumbnail and click **Save Changes**.

For lots more information on editing your videos, visit **https://www.youtube.com/yt/creators/en/tutorials.html**

https://www.youtube.com/watch?v=SdgJ-v76axQ

>> THE BOFFIN BIT <<

PREFERENCES

It's likely you will want to repeat certain edits to each one of your videos – perhaps to lighten the shots, or even to add your channel's logo onto the screen. You can avoid doing each of these actions from the beginning every time by saving them in **Preferences.**

For more information for Movie Maker go to: **http://windows.microsoft.com/en-GB/windows-live/movie-maker-settings-save-movie-how**

For iMovie go to: **http://macs.about.com/od/appleconsumersoftware/qt/Imovie-11-Advanced-Tools-How-To-Turn-On-Imovie-11s-Advanced-Tools.htm**

✳ SEVEN ESSENTIAL STEPS TO EDITING

1. Watch other YouTube videos and choose a style you like. Study their editing patterns, and how they move from one shot to the next.

2. Try creating specific videos, for example a dialogue scene, or an action scene, so you get experience of editing different kinds of videos.

3. Aim to edit each video down to about two minutes — you might think your ideas on shaping the perfect eyebrow are too good to miss, but anything longer just isn't going to hold people's attention.

4. Edit out the boring parts (pauses etc). This will give your video a faster and more interesting pace.

5. Don't leave your clips looking too dark and dreary. Use tools to brighten the video and match between shots.

6. Experiment using text and music to add originality to your videos.

7. And last but not least: your videos aren't finished until you've given them attention-grabbing titles and descriptions. Want to hit 1,000 views for your ball juggling video? Call it something like 'Ball skills like Rooney' rather than 'Ball juggling'. And make sure the thumbnail is as interesting as it can possibly be.

Pick five YouTube videos and see if they have used the following:

* Match cut
* Jump cut
* Split edit
* Transitions
* Effects (visuals and graphics)

How would you change the way you make your own videos based on this research?

DIY DUDE

Editing know-how

QUICK EXPERT SUMMARY

- Editing your video is as important as shooting it – perhaps more so.
- Choose the editing software that's right for you.
- Think about the edits you make, and what effect they have on the viewer. Have a clear plan in mind!
- Make your video look more professional using transitions and special effects – but don't go overboard!

IT'S GOOD TO SHARE

✳ HOW TO UPLOAD YOUR VIDEOS TO YOUTUBE

There's no point making interesting, well-edited videos if no one sees them — so now it's time to upload your video to YouTube and share it with other users.

>> THE BOFFIN BIT <<

COMPRESSION

Every video you upload will be reformatted (changed into a different file type) and compressed, basically shrunk by YouTube software to help it upload and stream more quickly and smoothly. This will make uploading quicker, and reduce the amount of space YouTube needs to store your video. It also means that the quality of your video will suffer – from a little to a lot depending on how you filmed it. So how do you keep your video looking great once it's compressed?

✳ Choose a simple background (no patterned wallpapers!).

✳ Keep your camera as still as possible (ideally on a tripod, if you have one).

✳ Shoot in close-up as much as you can.

✳ Ensure the video is well lit and properly exposed (which produces a sharper, clearer image when it's compressed).

For specific information on preferred file formats and sizes visit **www.youtube.com/help**

✳ 1. Log into YouTube and click the **Upload** button in the top right-hand corner of the site. The upload page will appear. From here, click the **Select Files to Upload** button to start uploading your content, or you can even drag and drop the video you want to upload. YouTube will begin converting and uploading the video.

✳ 2. If you want to control who watches the video, click the **Privacy** dropdown menu and select either **Public**, **Unlisted** or **Private**, and save changes. If you choose **Private**, you can then add the YouTube usernames or email addresses of the people you want to be able to view the file. (You can send up to 50 private invitations per video.) Videos uploaded as **Public** won't go live until you click the **Publish** button.

✳ 3. Tag your videos with descriptive words that will help potential viewers find your clips. This part is important — if you choose to make your videos public, without the right tags, no one's going to find them!

* **DO** choose tags that are specific. The more thoroughly you can describe the content of your video, the better.

* **DON'T** use the exact same tags as everyone else — your video will get buried that way.

* **DO** use a mixture of broad and specific tags. For example, as well as tagging your video as 'singing', add tags like 'freestyle rapping', or 'singing harmonies'.

www.youtube.com/upload

❝ Reaching out to [your] audience is equally as important as great content. By creating fantastic content and spending zero time [thinking about your] audience, you will not succeed on YouTube. You have to focus on [reaching your] audience as much as you focus on creating content. ❞

Robert Kyncl, YouTube Head of Content

SAY WHAT?

* **DO** choose keywords that apply to your video — 'music', 'comedy', 'prank' and so on.

* **DON'T** mislead viewers with keywords that aren't really relevant. Putting 'Justin Bieber' will get more views — but more annoyed 'Beliebers' than you want to encounter!

* **DO** tag videos with the names of people you mention, keywords related to events you talk about, and so on.

* **DO** use tags to create 'sets' of videos. Creating a unique tag and then applying it to each video that you want to keep together, will lead to more clicks through to your other related videos.

✳ 4. Want to upload videos that are longer than 15 minutes? You'll need to verify your account with Google, the owners of YouTube.

✳ UPLOADING VIDEO FROM YOUR PHONE

If you're uploading from an Android or iOS device (iPhone or iPad), you can upload through the YouTube app as follows:

1. Sign into the YouTube app and navigate to **My Channel**.

2. Touch the **Upload** icon at the top of the screen.

3. Select the video you want to upload from your device and touch the **Confirm** button.

4. Adjust the title, description, tags and privacy settings of your video.

5. Touch the **Upload** icon again.

To avoid being charged for data uploading, go to **Settings/Uploads** to restrict uploads to WiFi only.

REALITY CHECK

☑ **Swedish superstar**

Gamer Felix Kjellberg, better know to the world as PewDiePie, currently has a MASSIVE 28.4 million YouTube subscribers. 'Pewds', as he's known to his army of fans, plays video and mobile games and provides a running commentary – from jokes, to laughs, to squeaks of delight and gasps of surprise. What's more, his clip of 'Flappy Bird' in early 2014 turned the game into a worldwide sensation!

In 2012, PewDiePie signed with Maker Studios, a producer of online content that takes a share of advertising sales it places on clients' channels. The following year, his channel made an estimated £2.3 million, but PewDiePie believes his appeal is very simple. "What I and other YouTubers do is a very different thing," he explains. "It's almost like hanging around and watching your [friend] play videogames."

OFFICIAL FORM C-185A

✳ UPLOAD USING EMAIL

If you're not using Android or iOS, you can still upload videos direct to your channel using a special email address that's provided with your YouTube account.

Finding your unique email address

* On a desktop computer, go to YouTube settings.

* Under **Account Information**, find **Mobile Uploads**. You'll see an email address that looks something like ııııııııııııı@m.youtube.com

Can't see an email address? Click the **Create Mobile Profile** button and enter the information required. Click the **Create Profile** button to create an email address.

Uploading the video

* To upload the video, email it to the address above. You'll receive a confirmation email letting you know that your video was successfully uploaded.

* Edit the video and its settings by visiting YouTube from your desktop computer.

Imagine you're uploading videos on the following subjects:

 You miming and dancing to a Katie Perry song

 Your cat doing a somersault trying to catch a fly

 Your best friend doing tricks on a scooter

 Asking 20 people to name their most embarrassing moment.

List 15-20 tags you could use for each – from the general to the very specific. Use your imagination! Try and put yourself in the position of a YouTube viewer searching for a video on the subject you have filmed. What keywords would they use to find it?

Dude! :Ö.

QUICK EXPERT SUMMARY

- Uploading your video will reduce video quality. Bear this in mind when shooting!

- When you're uploading video, remember the privacy settings – who do you want to see your video?

- Tags and keywords are very important. Ignore them at your peril.

- Don't be afraid to upload from your phone. You can edit and tag the video later from a desktop if necessary.

GOING VIRAL

✳ MAKING FRIENDS, GAINING FOLLOWERS

You've chosen your topic, filmed, edited and uploaded your videos. They're great! So how do you get people to watch them? You can tell your friends, but how do you tell everyone else? It's time to start sharing your videos and become part of the larger YouTube community.

✳ EIGHT STEPS TO VIRAL SUCCESS

1. Make new videos at least once a week

To keep people coming back to your channel, you need to update it on a regular basis. If possible, stick to a schedule so people will know they can expect to see new content on a certain day. Let your viewers know when you're taking a break, if you're going on holiday for a couple of weeks, for example.

Setting a release schedule and sticking to it can help build a following. Think of it like a TV show — everyone looks forward to the next episode of their favourite show, and they know exactly when it's on air! You need to generate this buzz around your own channel.

VIRAL VIDEO

A viral video is so-called because it spreads like a virus from one person to the next. Virals (for short) become popular on Internet sites like YouTube, or by sharing links by email or via social media. Traditionally, viral videos were often funny homemade clips like 'Charlie Bit My Finger – Again!' but the most popular viral video ever is the music video for 'Gangnam Style' by Korean rapper PSY, which has been viewed over 2 billion times on YouTube!

https://www.youtube.com/watch?v=_0BIgSZ8s5M

https://www.youtube.com/watch?v=CH1XGdu-hzQ

In between new videos, spend time 'liking' other people's videos and promoting other content so your subscribers will have something to keep them occupied until your next video is ready.

Keep engaged with your subscribers throughout the week, not just on the day you post videos. Which leads us to...

2. Talk to your subscribers

Responding to every person who leaves you a comment is a great way to start building relationships with your subscribers. If someone leaves you a nice message, say thank you! If they ask for advice, give it. Spend a few hours after uploading a video responding to the comments that viewers make about it. These are your biggest fans — the ones eagerly awaiting your next video, and the ones brave enough to comment on it. Treat fans with respect and you'll see their numbers grow. Be genuine and friendly, and you'll attract more and more people. Here are a few other good ways to interact with your subscribers:

* Ask your viewers simple Yes/No questions, or to participate in votes about what you should film next. This will minimise negative feedback and promote discussion.

* Moderate the comments on your page. Nasty comments will detract from your channel and drive some viewers away. Remove offensive comments and report abusive users. This will help create a happier, friendlier environment for your regular viewers.

* Try to incorporate viewer comments into your videos. The best way to do this is to say you'll be taking the best subscriber suggestions, and including them in your next videos. Anyone who wants to participate will need to subscribe to your channel.

DIY DUDE
Removing subscribers from your channel

From time to time, you might need to remove a subscriber from your channel. Perhaps they're leaving rude comments for you or other subscribers. Here's how to do it:

1. Log into your YouTube account.

2. Under the **Subscriptions** and **Subscribers** section on the **My Account** page, click the **My Subscribers** link. A list of all your subscribers will appear.

3. Click the **Unsubscribe** button under the name of the person you want to remove.

Dude!

3. Use social media to get your name out there

Share your videos via other social networks like Facebook and Twitter. Encourage your friends, both online and offline, to pass your links on to others, but avoid spamming your social media networks with links to your channels. A friendly reminder now and then is good, but no one reacts positively to being hammered with links.

Promote your videos only to people you know. If you don't have a relationship with someone, don't ask them to watch or link to your video. Instead, work the relationships you already have and let the viewership build naturally. It's not going to happen overnight, but with persistence you'll see your views going up.

4. Watch other people's channels

YouTube is a community, and if you want to be popular, you need to participate. Interact with other people on their walls, via messages or on Twitter. Make sure you actually watch videos before leaving a comment. Give genuine *positive* feedback. People will know if you're being fake, especially if you spam them with a link to your channel (see above). When you're not actively maintaining your channel you should be watching other people's videos, interacting with other users, and browsing for like-minded content.

* Link to other users' content that you feel complements your own. This will help your channel show up on searches as related viewing.

* Try to maintain a schedule for adding links to other videos. Do this on days when you're not uploading your own videos. This will help break up the wait between your videos, keeping your viewers active on your channel.

* When liking other videos, make sure they're videos that you think will appeal to the greatest number of your subscribers as possible. You don't want to turn away your audience because no one likes the video you liked.

5. Tell your viewers to spread the word

Remind your viewers to like your videos, and suggest that they share them. These messages are best saved for the end of the video, after the important content has been viewed.

SAY WHAT?

" *Human beings don't want to just enjoy something by themselves. They want to share that emotion — they want everyone around them to enjoy it like they enjoy it or hate it like they hate it. That's what makes a video [go viral].* "

YouTuber Ray William Johnson

6. Collaborate with other content creators

Build relationships with other YouTubers in the same field as you. Agree to cross-promote each other's channels. You could even make guest appearances in each other's videos! Make sure that your viewers can easily find the channels that you are collaborating with by posting links to them.

7. Keep it fresh

If you're known for making prank videos, release a vlog talking directly with the audience, answering questions and responding to comments. This behind-the-scenes look will create a stronger bond with your audience and make them feel like they have an impact on your work.

If you have older content that your new viewers probably haven't seen, stick it in your feed so that everyone sees it on the front of your channel page. This can give your old videos increased viewing.

8. Respond to real world events

The media constantly creates hype around events throughout the year. These are known as 'tent pole' events. Think about what events are relevant to your subscribers, and how your programming can reflect that. 'How to choose the perfect Christmas gift' or even 'How to avoid Valentine's Day', are good examples.

Create videos leading up to the event to capitalise on pre-event searches. As anticipation grows for an event, more and more people will be searching for related content. Interact with your viewers throughout the process to keep them coming back to your channel. Consider increasing the amount of content you release in the build-up to these events to make the most of the increased traffic.

✳ MAKING MONEY ON YOUTUBE

We've talked a lot about the importance of doing something you enjoy when setting up a YouTube channel, and of course that should be your main motivation for becoming a YouTuber. However, it's now possible with the help of the YouTube Partner Programme to earn money from your channel too. YouTube runs an advertising programme called AdSense, which allows advertisers to place ads at the start of certain chosen videos. The advertisers are happy because they know that lots of people are seeing their adverts, and YouTubers who want to take part each receive a small amount of money for every view of the ads

on their channel. The amount of money that the advertisers pay (and therefore what you earn) is based on the popularity of the videos and the channel. To learn more, go to **https://support.google.com/youtube/answer/72902?hl=en**

DIY DUDE

Staying safe online

Dude!

Here are a few tips that will help keep your online experience happy and safe:

If you're a victim of cyberbullying, block the offender immediately (see p50) and tell an adult what has happened. Consider reporting the person to YouTube here: **https://support.google.com/youtube/answer/2801920?hl=en-GB**

Think carefully about the videos you post, and don't post anything you're unsure about. If in doubt, ask an adult's advice. Videos can be deleted, but once something is online it's possible for viewers to take screengrabs of what you've posted.

NEVER post your full name, the name of your school, or your address or phone number online.

If anyone makes you feel uncomfortable in the comments section of your videos, block them immediately and consider reporting them to the Child Exploitation and Online Protection Centre here **http://www.ceop.police.uk/safety-centre**

Always speak to a parent or teacher if you have any concerns.

Check out the site **https://www.thinkuknow.co.uk** for further advice. It's run by the UK government's Child Exploitation and Online Protection Centre (CEOP).

✳ ARE THERE ALTERNATIVES TO YOUTUBE?

YouTube is currently the undisputed biggest video website on the planet! Over 40 per cent of the world's Internet users visit **every month**, and 100 hours of video are uploaded every minute. But, if you're interested in the competition, you can check out:

Dailymotion

A French video-sharing website that's currently the 32nd most visited website in the world, with 2.2 billion video views per month, and 105 million unique monthly visitors. Although it's based in France, 85 per cent of the audience comes from abroad.

Vimeo

A US-based site with over 22 million registered users, and over 100 million unique visitors per month. Vimeo also runs a video on-demand service in the style of Netflix and Amazon Prime Video.

DIY DUDE

Spreading the word

Pick three smaller YouTube channels (with less than 5,000 subscribers each). Study how they promote their channels.

✳ Do they Tweet about it? Do they post on Facebook?

✳ How many other channels do they follow?

✳ How do they interact with their subscribers?

Make a checklist of their methods and try some for yourself.

REALITY CHECK

OFFICIAL REALITY CHECKER

THIS CARD CERTIFIES THAT
Melvin
IS OFFICIALLY APPOINTED
TO CHECK REALITY ON
BEHALF OF THE QUICK
EXPERT'S GUIDE

APPROVED

☑ The queen of YouTube

US YouTuber Jenna Marbles (real name Jenna Mourey) is a one-woman production line. She dreams up, stars in, films, edits and uploads all her own videos – often in a single day! And it's working! Her make-up tips video 'How to trick people into thinking you're good looking' has been viewed 58 million times, and she is currently the seventh most subscribed channel on YouTube.

Marbles is a great example of someone whose personality, ideas and delivery are more important than expensive cameras, lighting and professional production. Fans love the 'amateur' approach of her videos, which now include impressions (of Lady Gaga among others), dating advice and news on her own life's ups and downs. How does she describe her success? "I have fun in my house, by myself, and put it on the Internet."

https://www.youtube.com/
user/JennaMarbles

OFFICIAL FORM C-185/A

✳ BUILD YOUR OWN CHANNEL!

Finally, it's time to put all your new-found knowledge into action: it's time to build your own channel.

Step 1: Make some plans for your channel

Consider what your channel is going to be about. What are you interested in? What are your skills? Research what's already out there — how many people are doing it? How do they film their videos? How many subscribers do they have?

Think about how you can make your channel different. Would you wear your favourite football kit to appeal to that team's fans for your football skills channel? Would you replicate classic skills from professional players? Try to offer something different to your competition.

Ask friends what they would like to see. Decide how often you're able to post, and make a list of the skills you're planning to showcase. Will you have enough to keep a channel filled with content?

Step 2: Name your channel

Take your time coming up with a suitable channel name. Check that something similar isn't already in use. If it is, find an alternative or adapt it.

Think of a channel description that neatly sums up what you're planning to do.

Step 3: Design your channel

Consider the colours and layout you will use. Certain colours for your football skills channel will remind viewers of particular team kits — this could be a good or a bad idea!

Step 4: Plan your filming

Can you film the videos yourself, or do you need a friend to help?

Think about the kind of shots you will need. Are you filming in close-up? Are you using medium shots?

What camera are you filming on? Can you use a tripod so the image is steady?

What camera skills could help your channel stand out from its competitors?

Step 5: Edit your videos

Consider what editing software you're going to use — PC or Mac?

How long are your videos going to be? Try to keep them at two minutes or under.

What edits are you going to use — match cuts? Jump cuts? A combination?

Think about adding graphic effects and a soundtrack to your videos to make them more interesting.

Step 6: Upload and share

Naming and tagging your videos is ultra-important! Think about the searches you would make to find videos of specific skills. Include those in your video description.

Step 7: Go viral

Make sure you release regular videos. If your subscribers know you release a new video every Tuesday, for example, they'll keep coming back for more.

Interact with your subscribers — thank them for their interest, ask their advice about future videos, listen to their comments.

Watch other people's channels and praise what they do well. Consider collaborating on videos with other YouTubers making similar videos, to combine audiences.

Step 8: Keep doing it!

To be a successful YouTuber, you have to keep making videos. So what are you waiting for?

QUICK EXPERT SUMMARY

- Make a schedule of uploading new videos – and stick to it! Viewers will come back to your channel if they know you regularly upload new clips.

- Interact with your subscribers – listen to their comments, ask for their views.

- Watch other channels, and reach out to YouTubers you enjoy. Perhaps you can even collaborate?

- Use social media to spread the word about your channel – but don't spam!

- Think about real-world events you can cover on your channel. Lots of people will be searching them.

THE LAST WORD ON BEING A YOUTUBER

Having **dipped your toe** in the water of YouTubing, hopefully you can now **go forth** and create your own **successful video channel**. The most important thing to remember is to **have fun!**

>> USEFUL LINKS <<

※ **BULLYING/CYBERBULLYING**

http://www.bullying.co.uk

※ **CENTRE FOR INTERNET ADDICTION**

http://www.netaddiction.com

※ **CHILD EXPLOITATION AND ONLINE PROTECTION CENTRE (CEOP)**

http://ceop.police.uk

※ **EDITING SOFTWARE FOR MAC**

www.apple.co.uk/ilife

※ **EDITING SOFTWARE FOR PC**

http://www.adobe.com/uk/products/premiere-elements.html and

www.microsoft.com/downloads

※ **STAY SAFE ONLINE**

http://www.staysafeonline.org/stop-think-connect/tips-and-advice

※ **THINK U KNOW**

https://www.thinkuknow.co.uk — how to stay safe online

>> GLOSSARY <<

Adaptor — a device that's used to connect two pieces of electrical equipment.

Age-restricted content — content (usually videos) that are rated as only being suitable for people over a certain age.

Ambient lighting — table lamps, floor lamps etc. Subtle lighting with no spotlights.

Aperture — the opening on a camera or recording equipment through which light passes to create an image or video.

Collaborate — to work together with someone for a particular purpose.

Contagious — spreading very quickly from one person to another (see 'viral').

Cross-promote — to advertise someone else's channel in exchange for them advertising yours.

Customise — to make something more personal or particular to your own tastes or needs.

Exposure — the amount of light that hits the image sensor, controlled by the shutter speed and aperture.

Framing — how an image appears through a camera or camcorder's viewfinder.

Gain — the setting on your video camera that allows you to film in very low light.

Image stabilisation feature — a feature on a camera or camcorder that reduces the blurring of objects which can happen when a camera moves.

Intuitive — able to suggest information or subjects of interest based on past online behaviour, e.g. searches or purchases.

Officially licensed music — music that the copyright holder has given permission to be used for a specific purpose.

Portability — the ability to be easily carried.

Shutter speed — the amount of time the shutter is open, allowing light into the camera or recording device.

Social media — Twitter, Facebook etc; ways of communicating and sharing information using the Internet or mobile phones.

Spamming — sending out regular unwanted emails to people.

Tags — the labels added to videos which help people identify what the videos contain.

Teaser — something designed to raise people's interest and excitement.

Thumbnail — a small video 'window' showing one frame of video that aims to be representative of the content of the video.

Verify — to check or prove that something is true. To verify your email address, you are usually sent an email to that address, and asked to click a link to prove the email address is active and receiving mail.

Viral — something that spreads or becomes popular very quickly by being passed from one person to another online.

Vlogger — a video blogger; someone who records videos on a particular subject.

White balance — the adjustment of the brightness of the red, green and blue components of light, so the brightest object in the image appears white.